A
WORLD WAR TWO
SUBMARINE

Series Editor	David Salariya
Book Editor	Vicki Power
Design Assistant	Carol Attwood

Author:
Richard Humble has written over twenty two books on the history of ships, maritime exploration and naval history since his first book was published in 1971. Married with twin daughters, he lives and works in Devon.

Illustrator:
Mark Bergin was born in Hastings, in 1961. He studied at Eastbourne College of Art and has specialized in historical reconstruction since leaving art school in 1983.

First American edition published in 1991 by
Peter Bedrick Books
2112 Broadway
New York, NY 10023

Library of Congress Cataloging-in-Publication Data
Humble, Richard.
   A World War Two Submarine / Richard Humble : [illustrated by] Mark
Bergin. -- 1st American ed.
   (Inside story)
   Includes index.
   Summary: Text and cutaway illustrations depict how the crew lived
beneath the ocean in a submarine during World War II.
   ISBN 0-87226-351-7
   1. Submarines – History – Juvenile literature. 2. Seafaring life –
History – 20th century – Juvenile literature. 3. World War,
1939-1945 – Naval operations – Submarine – Juvenile literature.
[1. Submarines – History. 2. World War, 1939-1945 – Naval operations –
Submarine.] I. Bergin, Mark, ill. II. Title. III. Series: Inside story
(Peter Bedrick Books)
V857.H88 1991
359.9'3832 – dc20   91-16416
                                          CIP AC

Printed in Hong Kong by Wing King Tong Ltd.
91 92 93 94 95 5 4 3 2 1

A
WORLD WAR TWO
SUBMARINE

RICHARD HUMBLE   MARK BERGIN

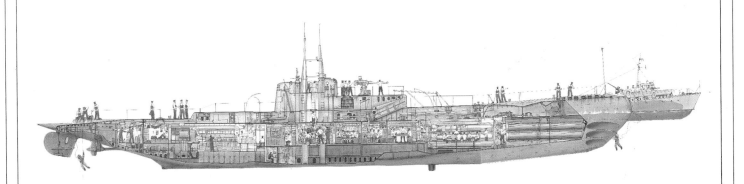

PETER BEDRICK BOOKS

NEW YORK

CONTENTS

INTRODUCTION

The deadliest warship of World War II was not the giant battleship with its mighty guns, nor the aircraft carrier with its fleet of aircraft. It was 'the enemy below', that unseen menace beneath the waves: the submarine.

Submarine attacks on merchant ships nearly won the war for Germany, and ensured that Japan would lose it. Even when the most powerful warships afloat stayed in home waters, far out of reach of enemy guns and bombs, submarines could find and sink them.

Life in a submarine was cramped, dirty and always dangerous. Every man aboard lived and worked in a world lit only by electricity, only breathing fresh air and eating hot meals when the submarine surfaced. It was quite usual for over half a submarine's crew never to see the sky from the day the submarine left harbor to the day it returned.

A special guide to one of the most extraordinary weapons of all time, this book shows how submarines came to be invented, how they work, and what it was like to work and fight in them between 1939 and 1945.

THE FIRST SUBMARINES

1. The pilot of *Turtle* (1776) had portholes just above the surface to see where he was going, and tubes to bring him fresh air. He is shown working the propellers and pumping out the ballast tank.

2. Another early submarine design was the American Robert Fulton's *Nautilus* (1800). It was hand-powered, and had a collapsible sail for moving on the surface.

3. *Argonaut* (1894) was American Simon Lake's idea for a wheeled diving-bell. With weights and tanks for diving and surfacing, it was designed to crawl across harbor floors as a working base for divers.

To make a submarine meant working out how to sink a ship deliberately, and also, of course, how to reverse the sinking process. By the middle of the 18th century, inventors had considered using pumps and flooding chambers to make a sealed and weighted boat dive and surface. But the Americans, in the War of Independence against Britain (1776-83), were the first to use such a craft to attack a surface warship with explosives.

David Bushnell's clumsy, wooden, man-powered *Turtle* was used only once, when it failed to fix an explosive charge to the British flagship *Eagle*. But it was the true forerunner of the modern fighting submarine.

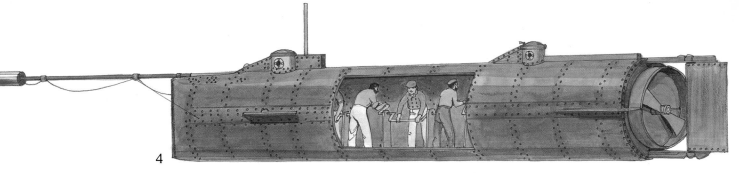

4

Another early submarine design, Robert Fulton's *Nautilus* (1800), failed to interest navies. But in the American Civil War (1861-65), the rebel Confederates attacked the US fleet with boats called 'Davids'. Most 'Davids' were hand-powered, moving just below the surface, ramming an explosive charge against the ship being attacked.

To store power for driving a submarine under water, the Briton George W. Garrett used tanks that held steam under high pressure (1879). But the best early submarine design belonged to John P. Holland: it had a gasoline engine for surface use and electric motors for underwater use.

6

6. **Designed** by George Garrett, *Resurgam* (1879) used pressurised steam under water.

4. The 'David' *H. L. Hunley* was the first underwater craft to sink a ship: the USS *Housatonic*, on February 17, 1864. But the blast also sank the *Hunley*.
5. **Caged mice** gave warning when the air grew dangerously foul.

5

Entry hatch

Torpedo tube

14 inch torpedo

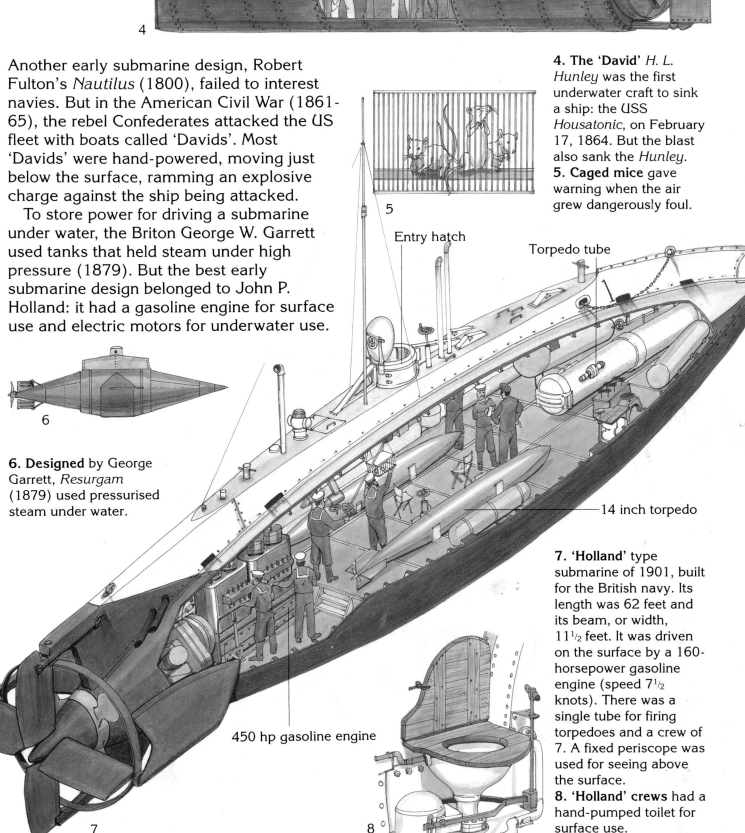

450 hp gasoline engine

7

7. **'Holland' type** submarine of 1901, built for the British navy. Its length was 62 feet and its beam, or width, 11½ feet. It was driven on the surface by a 160-horsepower gasoline engine (speed 7½ knots). There was a single tube for firing torpedoes and a crew of 7. A fixed periscope was used for seeing above the surface.
8. **'Holland' crews** had a hand-pumped toilet for surface use.

8

TWO WORLD WARS

Armed with torpedoes, submarines were no longer interesting novelties. They had become deadly weapons of naval warfare. The battleship remained the world's most powerful weapon until World War II, but even the strongest fleet of battleships went in fear of torpedo attacks by submarines. The tremendous blast of a torpedo below the waterline could cripple or sink the strongest warship afloat.

Arming submarines with guns in World War I enabled them to attack on the surface. Submarines were also used to lay mines in enemy waters. In both world wars, big submarines were built to operate like submersible cruisers, armed with guns and even carrying seaplanes in watertight hangars. Flotillas of German submarines

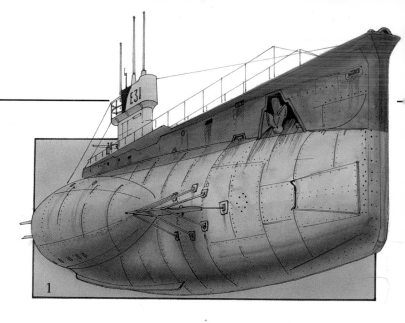

1. A British 'E' class boat of 1914, a successful class. It was 180 feet long, had 5 torpedo tubes (2 bow, 1 stern, 2 firing across the beam), a 12-pound gun and a crew of 30.

2. U-31, an ocean-going German U-boat of 1915, 212 feet long with 2 bow and 2 stern torpedo tubes, a $3\frac{1}{3}$ inch gun and a crew of 39.

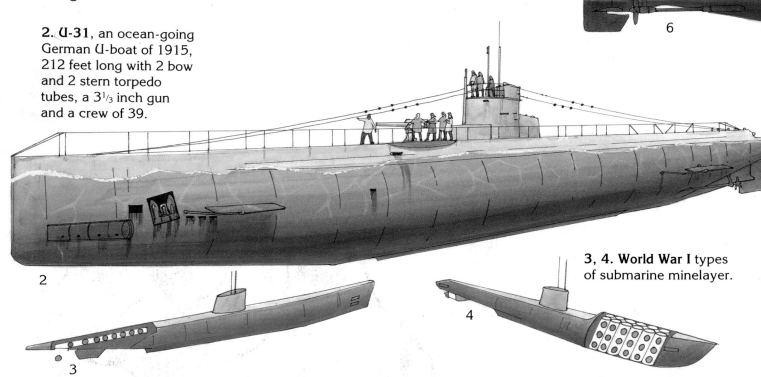

3, 4. World War I types of submarine minelayer.

(known as *Unterseeboote* or 'U-boats') sank so many merchant ships bound for Britain that Germany came close to victory in both 1917 and 1943.

The slow speed of the submarine's electric motors used underwater was overcome by building submarines with more powerful electric motors fed by much bigger electric batteries. The streamlined Type XXI U-boats of 1944-45 were designed to be faster below the surface than on it, to escape attacks by anti-submarine warships above.

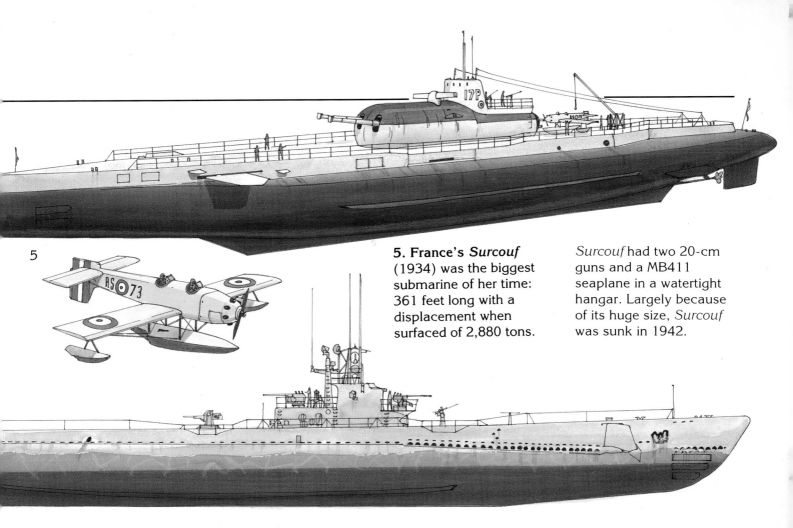

5. France's *Surcouf* (1934) was the biggest submarine of her time: 361 feet long with a displacement when surfaced of 2,880 tons.

Surcouf had two 20-cm guns and a MB411 seaplane in a watertight hangar. Largely because of its huge size, *Surcouf* was sunk in 1942.

6. American 'Gato' class, one of the most successful World War II types. Armed with 6 bow and 4 stern torpedo tubes, it was 314 feet long. Its diesels gave a surfaced speed of 20 knots and the crew numbered 80.

7. The German Type XXI U-boat was designed as a high speed submarine. It had an air-breathing snorkel to run submerged on diesels, and enlarged battery space for more speed on electric power. Built with a streamlined design for extra speed, the Type XXI submarine could travel at 16 knots submerged.

DESIGNING A SUBMARINE

Submarine designers begin by listing the tasks that the new boat will have to carry out. If it is to be an ocean-going submarine, it will need to store large quantities of fuel and must be able to dive deep. Small coastal submarines do not need these facilities. How many torpedo tubes is the boat to have, and how many spare torpedoes can be carried? Is the boat to have a gun for fighting on the surface, and will there be room for anti-aircraft guns as well?

All submarines consist of a pressure hull, which is supported on the surface by ballast tanks. These are flooded to dive and pumped empty to surface.

But there have to be holes in this strong pressure hull. There must be leak-proof hatches for getting in and out, and mountings for the torpedo tubes. All these openings need to be designed with special care.

Inside the pressure hull the crew lives and works, the engines and motors drive the submarine and provide its electricity. Though operated from inside, all the submarine's controls are outside the pressure hull. The controls are the rudder for steering, the hydroplanes for angling the boat up and down, and the vents, which open and shut to let water into and out of the ballast tanks for diving and surfacing.

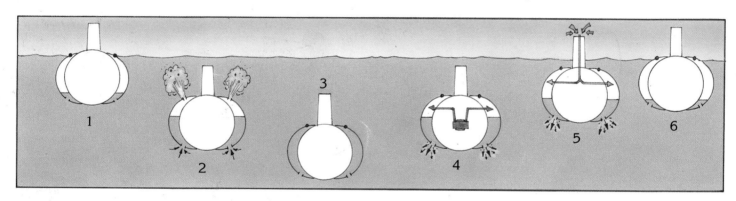

1. **Submarine** on surface, supported on air-filled ballast tanks with main vents shut.
2. **Submarine** submerging with main vents open and seawater entering ballast tanks.
3. **Submarine** submerged with ballast tanks full.
4. **Submarine** beginning to surface, with compressed air forcing seawater out of the ballast tanks.
5, 6. **As the conning tower** breaks surface the submarine levels off on its planes. A low pressure blower now blows the ballast tanks completely empty, and the engines are started.

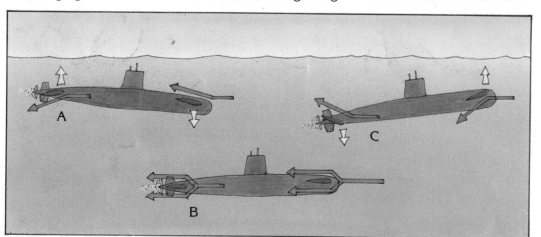

A submarine's hydroplanes act like horizontal rudders against the flow of water caused by the boat moving forward, tilting it downwards or upwards in the water. When angled down, the planes help force the bow under the surface.
A. Planes angled to dive.
B. Planes level.
C. Planes angled to rise.

Ballast tanks
1. Internal ballast tank.
2. Saddle tanks –
pressure hull flanked by
main ballast tanks,
common to most World
War II submarines.
3. Partial double hull.
4. Double hull.

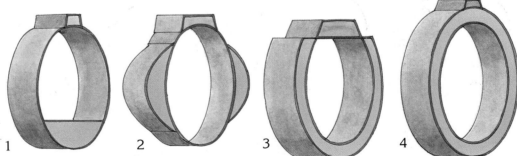

1   2   3   4

After diving, a
submarine must be
trimmed by adjusting the
weights of water in
internal compensating
tanks, then kept level
by pumping water
between internal
trimming tanks.
A. Normal surface trim.
B. Submarine diving.
C. Periscope depth trim.

BUILDING A SUBMARINE

World War II submarines were usually ordered in batches of each type, or class. How many were built each year depended on the capacity of the shipyards and the need for other types of warship.

As with all ships, building a submarine began with laying down the keel on a line of wooden stocks. Above the keel rose the circular frames of the pressure hull. Once this framework was completed and plated over, the ballast tanks and lighter plating of the outer skin, or casing, were added.

The engines, planes, rudder and torpedo tubes were built in while the submarine was still on the stocks. All the other internal fittings were added after the submarine had been launched and towed to a special fitting-out berth for completion.

1. Red-hot steel plate, made in the roar of a foundry rolling-mill.

2. On the stocks: plating covers the frames of a new submarine.

2

With time allowed for sea trials and the correction of faults, a submarine could be built, fitted out, and ready for action within 18 months. The British 'S' class *Storm* was laid down on June 23, 1942 and launched on May 18, 1943. *Storm* was commissioned as a warship, manned by her first power trials on August 10 and her first dive on August 21. After two more months of working-up or accustoming the crew to their new ship, *Storm* sailed for her first war patrol on November 11, 1943.

3. Using a template to check the curve before the plate is shaped by a hydraulic press.

3

4

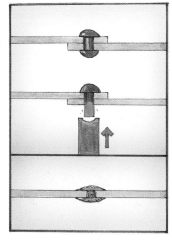

5

4. Shipyard workers of the 1940's. On every dive, the submariner entrusted his life to the work of the boat's builders. These formed a small army of craftsmen: riveters, welders, electricians, and carpenters for the inside furnishings.

5. Riveting and welding. The traditional way of securing steel plates was to overlap them, drill through the overlap, and fix them with a rivet. Welding, which melts the parts together, makes a stronger join.

Unlike welded boats, riveted submarines creaked under pressure, warning their crews, when water pressure became dangerous.

6

6. The launch of a British 'T' class submarine, of which 53 were built between 1937 and 1945. Like most British submarines, the boats of the 'T' class were built by British shipyards: Vickers Armstrong at Barrow-in-Furness, Cammell Laird at Birkenhead, Scotts at Clydebank, and by the Royal Navy yards at Portsmouth, Chatham and Devonport.

INSIDE A SUBMARINE

The next six pages show sections of a typical medium-sized submarine of World War II, the British 'S' class submarine. The shaded area on the diagram opposite shows the stern section of the submarine described on these two pages.

The basic equipment and way of life shown here were common to most submarines of the period, and submarines of all types faced similar technical and operational problems.

The 'S' class submarine displaced 735 tons on the surface and 935 tons submerged, and was powered by 2-shaft diesel and electric motors.

Its top surfaced speed was 16 mph, or 13¾ knots. The submarine was armed with 6 21 inch bow torpedo tubes, a 3 inch 'disappearing' or retractable gun which could be lowered into a well, and a machine gun. The normal crew was 36 men.

This view of the tapering stern section shows the rudder and stern hydroplanes, supported on a vertical fin. A diver has gone down to inspect the propeller blades and check them for possible damage. Stokers of the Engineer Branch are seen below, relaxing off watch, beneath the after escape hatch. The diesel engine is running, recharging the submarine's electric battery.

1. Rudder.
2. Stern hydroplanes.
3. Aft trimming tank.
4. Starboard propeller.
5. Trimming tank.
6. Steering shaft.
7. Emergency steering unit.
8. Stokers' accommodation.
9. After escape hatch.
10. Motor room (electric).

11. Lubricating oil tank.
12. Engine room (diesel).
13. Oil fuel tanks.
14. Retractable bollards.
15. Diesel exhaust.
16. Engine room hatch.

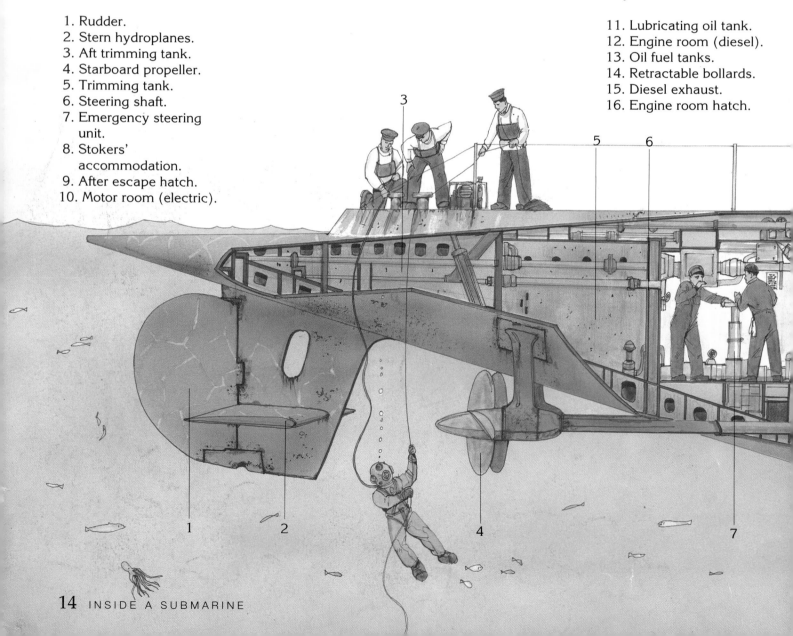

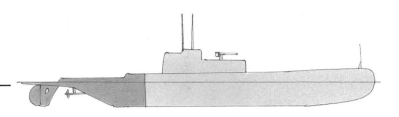

This part of the ship was the domain of the Engineer Branch. Its main duty was to keep the engines running, delivering thrust for the propellers and power to charge the battery which provided electric power and lighting for the entire submarine. The chief engineer, responsible for every system throughout the submarine, was the engineer officer: usually a lieutenant (E). Under him, the engines were tended by a chief engine room artificer (CERA), who supervised a team with 5 or 6 ERAs, a stoker petty officer, and 6 or 7 leading stokers and other stokers.

One difficult task of the Engineer Branch was to find the fault if one of the diesels was not running smoothly. Such a problem might be caused by a faulty piston, which would then have to be disconnected from the crankshaft and 'slung' at the top of its stroke. The engine would continue to run while repairs were made. The diesel engine and electric motor driving each propeller shaft were linked to the shaft by clutches. To run on electric motors, the diesels were disengaged by the engine clutches between each diesel and motor. The tail clutches disengaged the propellers during battery charging with the submarine stationary.

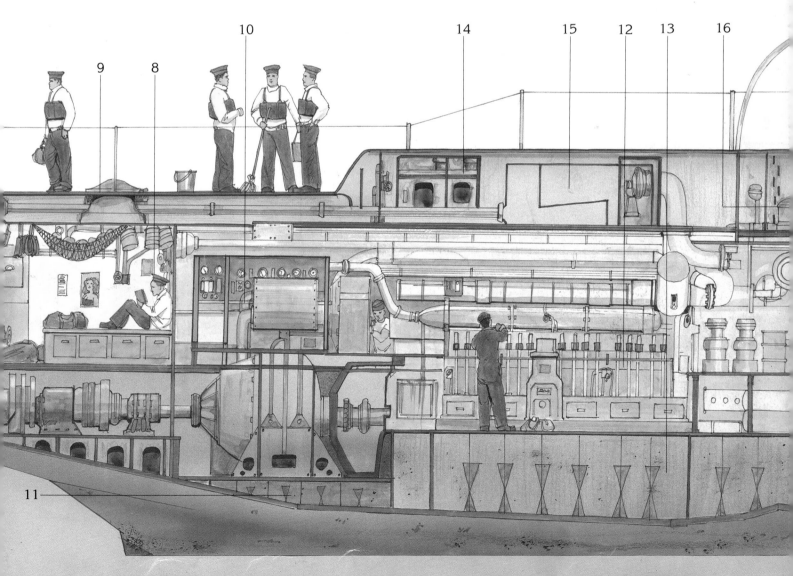

MIDSHIPS

1. Compressed air reservoir.
2. Indicator buoy.
3. Conning tower.
4. W/T (wireless telegraph) mast.
5. Bridge.
6. Periscope support standards.
7. Exterior steering unit.
8. Shells for gun.
9. Officer's cabin.
10. W/T office.

11. Wells for periscopes.
12. Control room.
13. ERAs' mess.
14. No. 1 battery.
15. 3 inch gun.
16. Folding boat.
17. Torpedo loading rails.
18. Seamen's mess.
19. Petty officers' mess.
20. Officers' wardroom.
21. No. 2 battery.
22. Sonar transmitter.
23. Spare torpedoes.

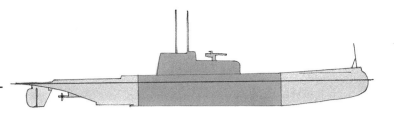

The midships section contained the submarine's brain, eyes, ears and voice. The control room was the brain, from which practically everything in the submarine was controlled. From here the captain or the officer of the watch, while scanning the surface through the periscope, could know exactly what was happening throughout the submarine. And it was in the control room that each attack was planned and directed.

Above the control room was the bridge from where the submarine was commanded and a constant lookout was kept while it was on the surface. (Radar was fitted in few submarines before 1943.) From the bridge, orders were passed below by voicepipe.

If the control room was the brain and the periscopes and surface lookouts were the eyes, hearing was provided by the sonar (called 'Asdic' in the British service) receiver. This detected the engine and propeller noises of other ships. And the submarine's voice, through which it kept in touch with its base and other warships and received its orders, was the radio (wireless telegraph, or W/T).

Along the bottom of the submarine was stored the boat's 'life blood': fuel and lubricating oil for the diesels, battery cells for the electric motors, and compressed air.

15

17

16

19   21   20   1   18   23

FORE ENDS AND BOW TUBES

Forward of the seamen's mess, where the men shared their living quarters with the bulky spare torpedoes in their racks, was the compartment known as the 'fore ends'. This led in turn to the tube space and the rear doors of the torpedo tubes, closed at their outer ends by the bow caps.

Careful checks were needed to guard against the accidental opening of a tube's rear door and bow cap at the same time, which could flood and sink the submarine. This happened to *Thetis* on her first dive in June 1939, when the vital hole to the test cock, which shows whether the tube is flooded or empty, had been painted over.

The crew was supervised by the coxswain, a chief petty officer responsible to the first lieutenant for the discipline, cleanliness and smooth running of the boat. Apart from the Engineer Branch, many other trades were represented in the crew of a submarine. There were electrical specialists, wireless telegraphists, a signalman, torpedomen, a gun-layer, sonar operators and a cook.

Every man had his special post when the crew went to 'Diving Stations', and some had other duties during torpedo attacks or gun actions. Nearly all seamen served as surface lookouts, as helmsmen at the steering wheel, and manning the hydroplane controls.

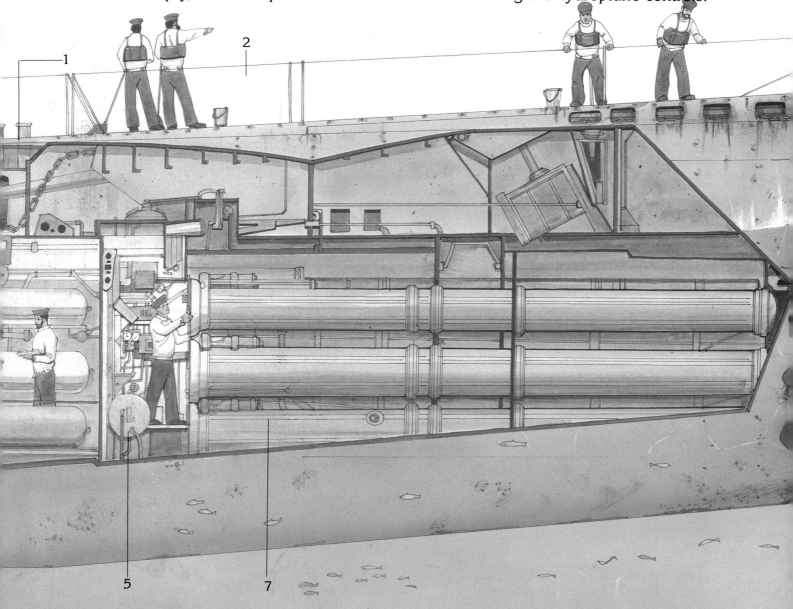

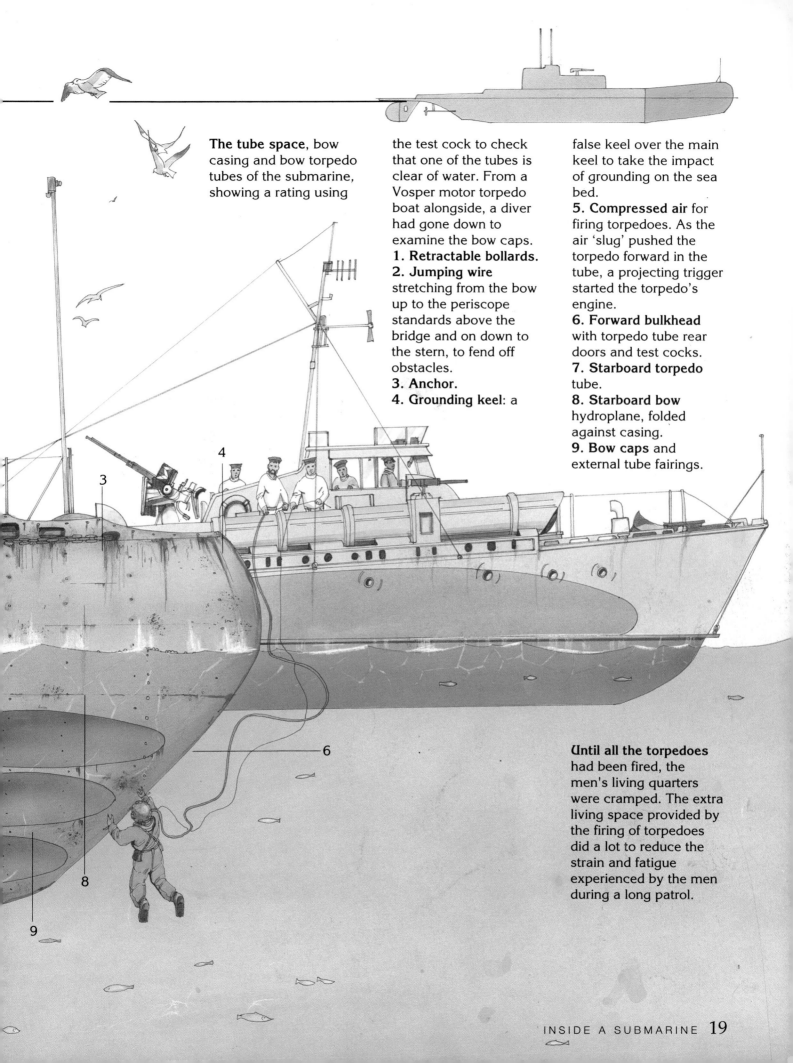

The tube space, bow casing and bow torpedo tubes of the submarine, showing a rating using the test cock to check that one of the tubes is clear of water. From a Vosper motor torpedo boat alongside, a diver had gone down to examine the bow caps.

1. Retractable bollards.

2. Jumping wire stretching from the bow up to the periscope standards above the bridge and on down to the stern, to fend off obstacles.

3. Anchor.

4. Grounding keel: a false keel over the main keel to take the impact of grounding on the sea bed.

5. Compressed air for firing torpedoes. As the air 'slug' pushed the torpedo forward in the tube, a projecting trigger started the torpedo's engine.

6. Forward bulkhead with torpedo tube rear doors and test cocks.

7. Starboard torpedo tube.

8. Starboard bow hydroplane, folded against casing.

9. Bow caps and external tube fairings.

Until all the torpedoes had been fired, the men's living quarters were cramped. The extra living space provided by the firing of torpedoes did a lot to reduce the strain and fatigue experienced by the men during a long patrol.

UNIFORMS

Strict uniform regulations made no sense aboard submarines. It was impossible to keep clothing clean for long; there was no spare water for laundry, and very little for personal washing. Dirt, oil and grease were unavoidable on a submarine patrol, during which clothes became increasingly damp and filthy. Yet the first lieutenant and coxswain would always insist on the crew keeping as clean as possible. When returning to base after a long patrol, submarine crews made it a point of honor to spruce up.

Dress in submarine crews depended very much on where the boat was serving. In cold northern waters, men wore several layers of warm clothing. In the tropics, the engine room crew usually worked stripped to the waist, and between patrols the men were encouraged to get as much sun as they could to combat skin problems.

1

2

3

1. British lieutenant, in peaked cap, with a seaman wearing the heavy roll-neck sweater of the British submarine service; his cap tally reads 'H. M. Submarines'. In the background is a stoker wearing overalls.

2. The Americans. Officer in US Navy khaki shirt and trousers, with a machinist's mate in blue shirt and denim trousers.

3. Some British sleeve badges, indicating rank and trade. Top to bottom: badge of submariners of HMS Dolphin at Gosport; the badge of a petty officer; the badge of a gunner's mate; a leading torpedoman's badge; a range taker's badge.

4. German U-boat men. At left, a U-boat *Kapitanleutnant* (equivalent to the British and American lieutenant-commander) in typically worn and grubby blue reefer jacket and uniform cap, with a lookout preparing for duty, wearing rough-weather coat. Behind them are petty officers.

Right, top to bottom: officer's cap; German Navy eagle badge (worn on the right breast); metal U-boat war badge; chief petty officer's rank badge; the chevron of a *Matrosenhauptgefreiter* or leading seaman, a torpedo specialist.

Right and below: U-boat emblems. *U-124*'s edelweiss blossom, *U-201*'s snowman, *U-552*'s dashing devil, and *U-338*'s kicking donkey.

One submarine captain recalled that he did not undress for weeks on end while on patrol. But nobody noticed, as everyone smelled alike! At the end of each patrol came the glorious moment when each crew member stripped off his layers of clothing for a long, hot bath. Under the last layer, his body would be covered with a fine white powder: the skin's cells that the body constantly sheds, but which in normal life fall invisibly away.

5. British 'Jolly Roger', flown after successful patrols: bars for ships sunk by torpedo, stars for sinkings by gunfire, and dagger for special missions.

SLEEPING AND EATING

Submarine crews spent most of each patrol submerged at 'watch diving'. The crew was divided into three watches, each of which spent two hours on duty and four hours off. Most submariners were encouraged to sleep when off watch, because this used less air.

Officers and petty officers had bunks, but even the biggest submarines lacked enough bunks for the whole crew. Men would sling hammocks in every available space, or simply bed down on the deck, on or under tables, or on locker tops.

Meals aboard submarines were governed by the diving sequence. There might be a cooked bacon, fish or egg dish for early breakfast before diving; cold lunch and tea were usually eaten submerged; usually the one hot meal of the day was cooked on the surface during battery charging. All too often, rough weather or an emergency dive meant that the men's only hot meal of the day ended up on the deck.

In British submarines, a major highlight of the daily round was the issue of the daily tot of rum for the men. Officers never drank alcohol at sea.

1

2

1. **A submarine** cook in his galley, with a hot meal ready to serve. The galley was usually located forward of the control room, with the cook serving as one of the gun crew during action.

The galley was small and used electricity for cooking. Very little fresh food could be carried. Cooks were trained to bake fresh bread and get as much variety as they could from a wide range of canned foods.

2. **A typical day's menu** aboard a submarine of 1941. **Breakfast**: Grapefruit, cornflakes, buttered eggs. **Lunch**: Canned soup, cold ham, fresh tomatoes, cold boiled potatoes, tangerine. **Tea**: Honey, jam or syrup on bread or biscuits. **Dinner**: Scotch broth, veal, boiled potatoes, canned beans, pineapple and custard.

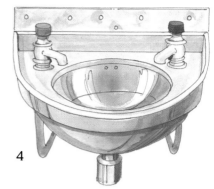

4

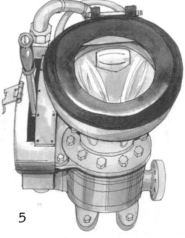

5

3. Even with a 'hot bunk' rota – men coming off watch taking the bunk of their relief – there were not enough bunks for the crew.

4. Wash basin, often banned to save water.
5. Pressure operated toilet, needing careful use to avoid 'getting your own back'!

6. Highlight of the British submariner's day: enjoying the tot of rum. The men's traditional toast was 'Stand fast the Holy Ghost'!

AT THE PERISCOPE

Submarines usually had two periscopes, both about 35 feet high. Their tubes were made of bronze to resist corrosion, and were raised and lowered by hydraulic power. When lowered, the periscopes rested in wells which were sunk through the deck of the control room.

Most periscope sightings were made with the search periscope, set for high power (magnifying by 6). The search periscope tapered from $9\frac{1}{2}$ inches to 4 inches at the tip. It had bifocal lenses, and could be used on low power (magnifying by $1\frac{1}{2}$) to give a wider field of view.

The slimmer attack periscope was designed to make as little wake as possible when raised; it tapered from $7\frac{1}{2}$ inches to 2 inches. Though harder for enemy lookouts to see, it also transmitted less light, and submarine captains would use the search periscope for as long as they dared when closing in on a target.

A wise captain would rarely use the search periscope closer to enemy lookouts than $2\frac{1}{4}$ miles on a calm day. The higher the periscope lens was above the water, the more you could see – which led most submarine captains to agree that if you could see clearly, you were almost certainly showing too much periscope!

keeping the submarine properly trimmed. His attention is fixed on the depth gauge and the bubble in the inclinometer, which shows any change in the submarine's attitude. Any hint of a loss of trim must be promptly and smoothly corrected. A sudden lurch upwards will expose too much

periscope. A lurch downwards will dip the periscope below the surface, leaving the captain 'blind'.

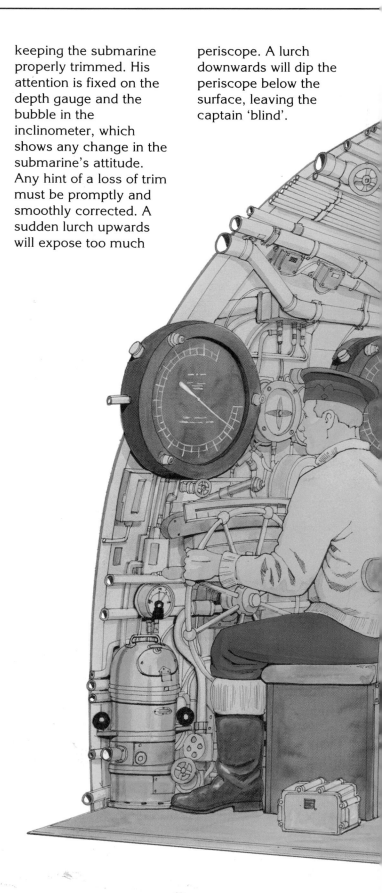

On one of his regular periscope searches, the officer of the watch in this patrolling submarine has sighted a suspicious mast and called the captain to the control room. Rolling fully clothed from his bunk, the scruffily-dressed captain has taken over the search periscope to see for himself.

On the left sit the two planesmen, controlling the angle of the hydroplanes as the submarine moves slowly on electric power at periscope depth. At the periscope, which from now on will only be raised at brief intervals to show as little as possible, the captain calls out the type of target, its apparent speed, distance and bearing, and orders his own course and speed changes.

Behind the captain stands the first lieutenant in cap and reefer jacket, with the vital task of

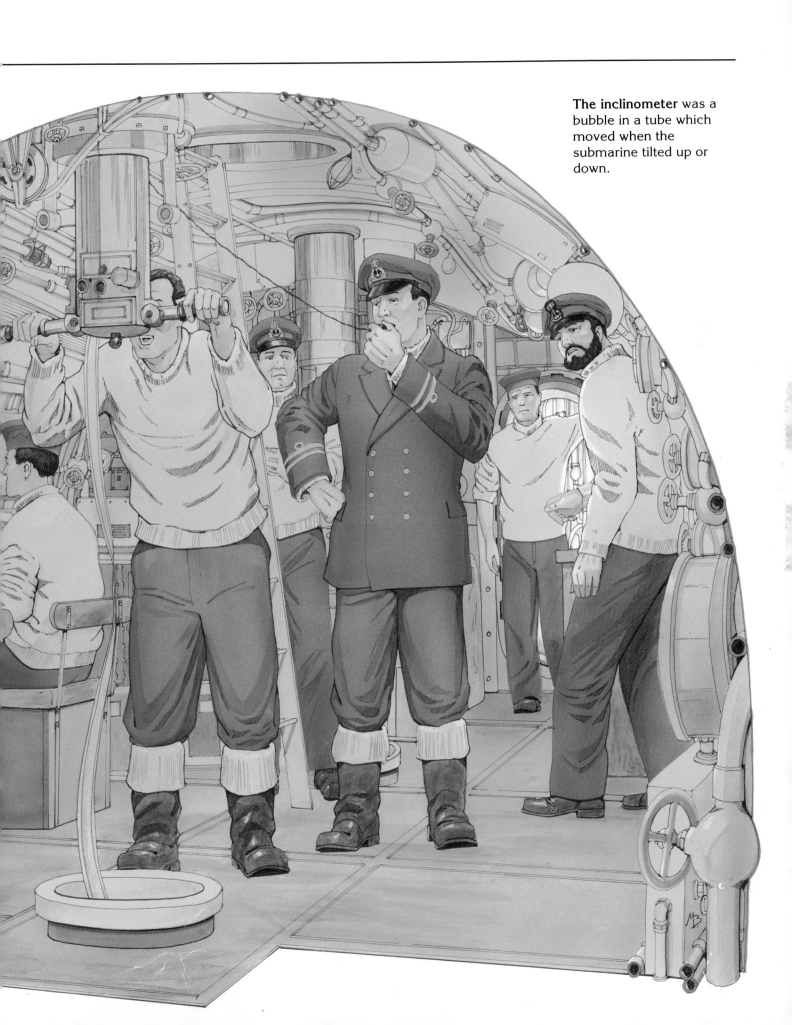

The inclinometer was a bubble in a tube which moved when the submarine tilted up or down.

SONAR

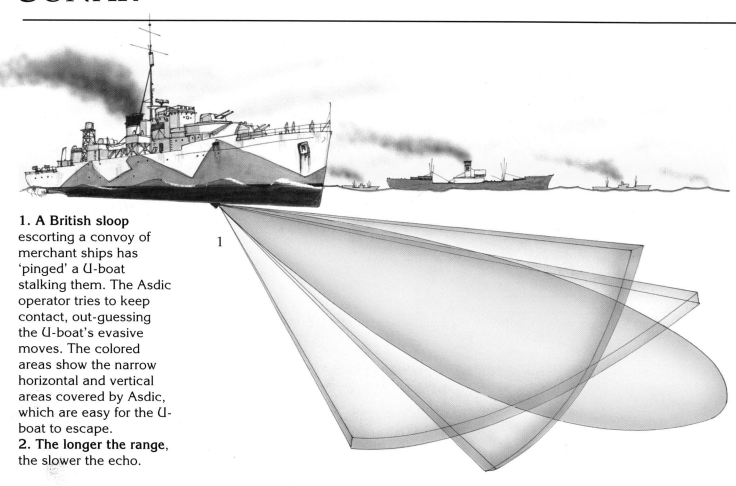

1. A British sloop escorting a convoy of merchant ships has 'pinged' a U-boat stalking them. The Asdic operator tries to keep contact, out-guessing the U-boat's evasive moves. The colored areas show the narrow horizontal and vertical areas covered by Asdic, which are easy for the U-boat to escape.

2. The longer the range, the slower the echo.

Known today by the word sonar ('from sound navigation and ranging'), the most useful tool for hunting submarines from the surface was first called Asdic. This word used the initials of the Anti-Submarine Detection Investigation Committee, set up late in World War I to find a method of locating submarines under water.

Developed between the wars, Asdic is an echo-ranging system. It uses a sound pulse, or 'ping', which is transmitted through the water. On hitting an underwater object, an echo comes back.

The transmitting ship then steers to 'run down' the Asdic contact. When the ship passes over the contact, 'ping' and echo make an almost simultaneous note. This is the moment to drop depth charges, which explode at the contact's estimated depth.

Aboard the hunted submarine, the 'ping' could be heard as a metallic tapping, which the submarine captain would try to escape by dodging outside the range of the Asdic.

The Germans developed a decoy called *Bold*, which formed a mass of bubbles that returned an echo. But expert Asdic operators soon learned to tell the difference between *Bold*, whales and genuine U-boat echoes.

A DAY IN THE LIFE OF A SUBMARINE

1. Torpedomen servicing torpedoes. Any fault in these complicated mechanisms could make them miss their target.

2. The next hot meal takes shape in the galley – maybe canned sausages, if the fresh meat has been used up.

3. Saving the last of the fresh bread. Cut off the moldy bits, sprinkle with condensed milk, heat up, and presto!

4. On the surface, with sky and horizon clear: time to find out why those bow planes are getting so stiff.

5. Approaching base, a cleaning party tackles oil streaks with 'softers and strongers' – soft soap and soda.

6. Battery check for loose connections, and maybe topping-up the cells with distilled water if the level has dropped.

7. 'Up Spirits', and the daily tot tastes better after cleaning up last night's supper, which got dropped on the deck.

8. Every submarine had some dripping pipes, for which the only answer was placing trays to catch the drips.

9. Trays of soda-lime absorbed at least some of the carbon dioxide breathed out into the air during a long dive.

10. Submarine crew and officers spent much of their free time playing highly competitive board games.

11. Dirt, grease, sweat and not a little bad language: repairing a faulty diesel piston in the engine room.

12. Torpedo firing drill: checking that the tube is flooded before firing a 'test slug' of compressed air, simulating a torpedo.

THE BREATH OF LIFE

Access to the surface was a matter of life or death, and not only in times of disaster when submarine escape systems were put to the test. Like whales, diesel-electric submarines had to surface regularly because of the need for air, both for men and machinery. Diesels could only be run on the surface to recharge the electric battery, while fresh sea air ventilated the boat and swept fumes away. And it was only on the surface that a submarine captain, using a sextant to 'shoot' the sun by day or stars by night, could confirm his position for accurate navigation.

Escaping from a submarine, usually after being sunk in shallow water by accidental collision, was difficult. Survival usually depended on being close to an escape hatch.

1. U-boat captain taking a star sight.

Snorkel head

2. The *schnorchel*, or snorkel, was a German air-breathing device. But if the snorkel jammed shut, the diesel engines would suck the air out of the submarine within seconds. The engines would eventually stop for lack of air, but not before the violent drop in air pressure had caused extreme discomfort and head pains to the crew.

A. Air entering.
B. Sea level.
C. Water separator.
D. Fresh air.
E^1. Exhaust gas.
E^2. Exhaust gas.
F. Hinged extending tube.

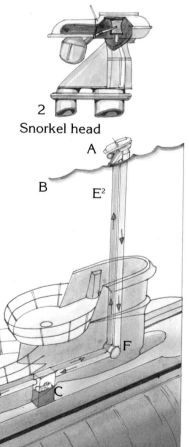

3. The British DSEA (David Submerged Escape Apparatus), an oxygen-breathing device, was also used to train frogmen divers. A canister of soda-lime 'Protosorb' in the breathing-bag absorbed carbon dioxide.

4. Used on U-boats, the German *Tauchretter* ('dive rescuer') used the same principle.

DIESEL AND BATTERY

1. **In full voice**, the 2 1,250 bhp (brake horsepower) Vickers diesels in the engine room of a 'T' class submarine. This was the biggest and most powerful British type built during World War II. The tremendous volume of air sucked in by the diesels helped ventilate the entire submarine. When the oxygen level of the air was low after a long dive, it could be difficult to coax the diesels to start until enough fresh air had found its way into the intakes.

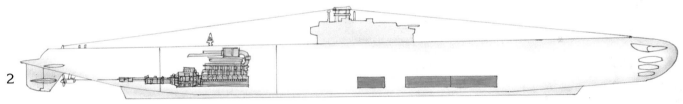

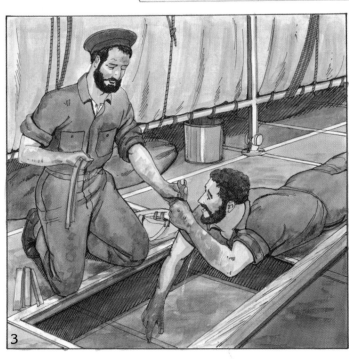

2. **Machinery** and battery layout, British 'T' class.
3. **Battery cell check.** When the electric motors were run at full speed submerged, the battery only lasted about an hour. Used at low speed, it would last about 36 hours.

The submarine's main power plant consisted of two diesel engines which turned the propeller shafts. Astern of the diesels were the electric motors.

On the surface, the motors were disconnected electrically and revolved freely on the shafts as the diesels turned them. On diving, the diesels were stopped and the engine clutch, between the diesels and the motors, was disengaged. This left the motors turning the shafts, using power from the battery, which had been recharged for about six hours a day while on the surface.

FIGHTING AN ATLANTIC GALE

Shown here is a U-boat running on the surface during an Atlantic gale. Many merchant ships, escorts and submarines operating in the North Atlantic during World War II were badly damaged and some surface ships were even sunk by violent weather. The surge of the waves could still be felt even when a submarine had dived as deep as 82 feet. One U-boat captain describes just how bad storm conditions could be:

'While trying to run before the storm at full speed, the boat dived twice. By blowing tanks, putting my helm hard over and reducing speed I managed to hold her reasonably well on the surface. To remain on the bridge was impossible. Within 30 minutes the captain and lookouts were half-drowned. Five tons of water poured into the boat in no time through the conning tower hatch, the voice-pipe and the diesel ventilating shaft.'

On the surface, apart from the captain or the officer of the watch, there were usually two lookouts. In really bad weather they had to use the naked eye. Even the Zeiss binoculars used by U-boat crews were useless when seas were breaking over the bridge.

On one British submarine battered by gales, all five pairs of lookout binoculars on board were flooded and rendered useless by torrents of seawater breaking over the bridge. All had to be taken to pieces and dried below by a technician.

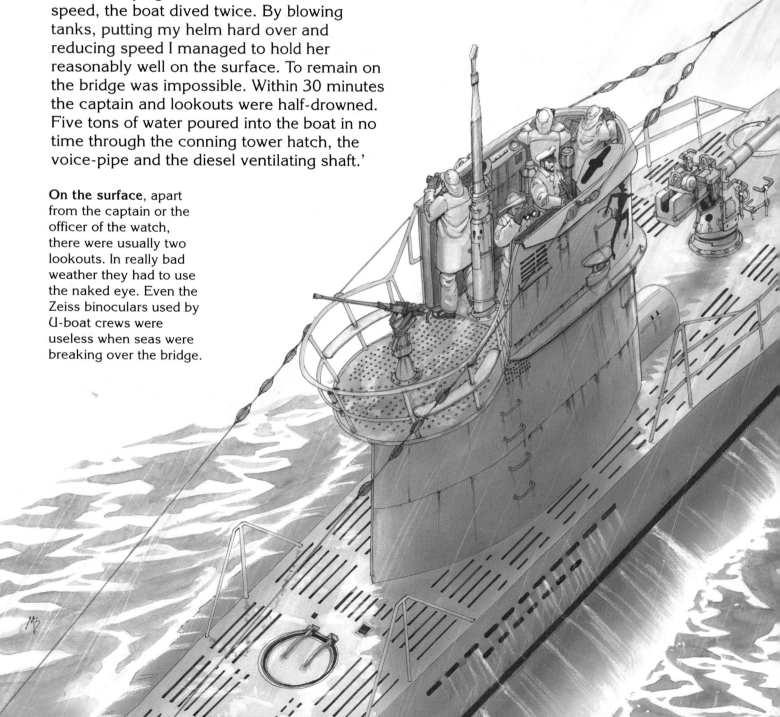

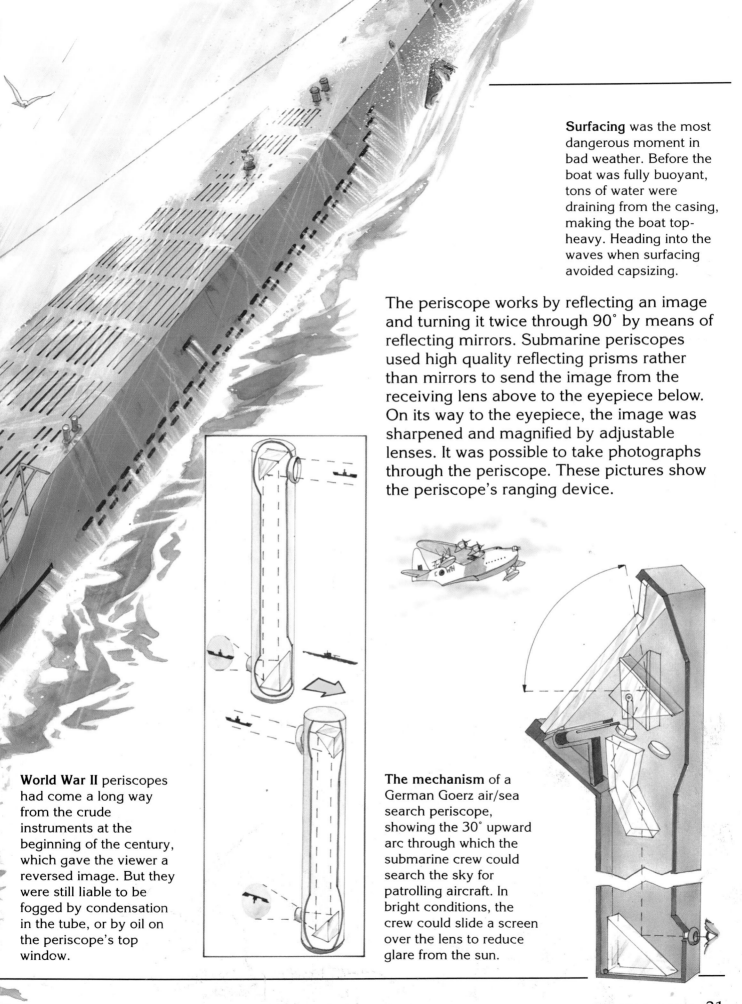

Surfacing was the most dangerous moment in bad weather. Before the boat was fully buoyant, tons of water were draining from the casing, making the boat top-heavy. Heading into the waves when surfacing avoided capsizing.

The periscope works by reflecting an image and turning it twice through 90° by means of reflecting mirrors. Submarine periscopes used high quality reflecting prisms rather than mirrors to send the image from the receiving lens above to the eyepiece below. On its way to the eyepiece, the image was sharpened and magnified by adjustable lenses. It was possible to take photographs through the periscope. These pictures show the periscope's ranging device.

World War II periscopes had come a long way from the crude instruments at the beginning of the century, which gave the viewer a reversed image. But they were still liable to be fogged by condensation in the tube, or by oil on the periscope's top window.

The mechanism of a German Goerz air/sea search periscope, showing the 30° upward arc through which the submarine crew could search the sky for patrolling aircraft. In bright conditions, the crew could slide a screen over the lens to reduce glare from the sun.

BRINGING TORPEDOES ABOARD

The submarine's value as a long range ship-sinker ended when all its torpedoes had been fired, unless it was in waters where its gun(s) could be used. Submarines sailed on patrol with all torpedo tubes loaded and at least one reload torpedo for each tube. As each weapon weighed about 1.5 tons, the firing of each torpedo made a considerable change to the submarine's trim. Though much of the lost weight was replaced by the natural flooding of the tube and by flooding a tank between the tubes, the remainder was corrected by pumping water between the trimming tanks.

Torpedoes were brought inside the pressure hull through the fore hatch, which was specially designed for the purpose. The torpedo was guided below along curved rails.

The British submarine *Tiptoe*, shown taking on torpedoes between patrols. Built by Vickers, *Tiptoe* belonged to the third group of 'T' boats, launched on February 25, 1944, displacing 1,321 tons surfaced and 1,571 submerged.

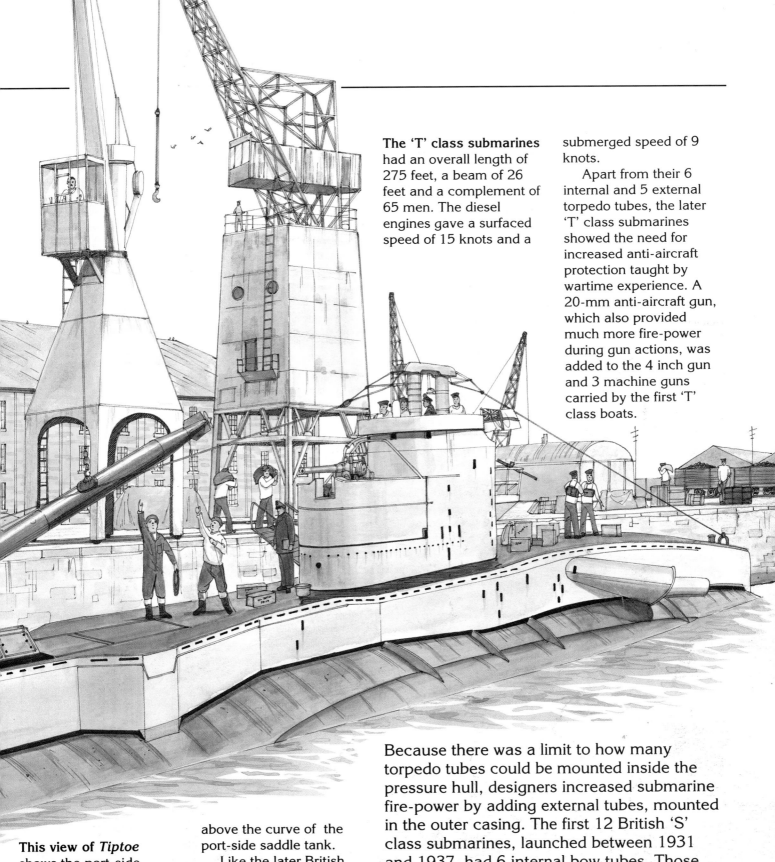

The 'T' class submarines had an overall length of 275 feet, a beam of 26 feet and a complement of 65 men. The diesel engines gave a surfaced speed of 15 knots and a submerged speed of 9 knots.

Apart from their 6 internal and 5 external torpedo tubes, the later 'T' class submarines showed the need for increased anti-aircraft protection taught by wartime experience. A 20-mm anti-aircraft gun, which also provided much more fire-power during gun actions, was added to the 4 inch gun and 3 machine guns carried by the first 'T' class boats.

This view of *Tiptoe* shows the port-side external bow tube cap above the waterline. Further aft can be seen the streamlined fairing or covering of the port-side external stern tube, above the curve of the port-side saddle tank.

Like the later British 'S' class submarines, the hull strength of the later 'T' class boats was greatly improved by the complete use of welded construction.

Because there was a limit to how many torpedo tubes could be mounted inside the pressure hull, designers increased submarine fire-power by adding external tubes, mounted in the outer casing. The first 12 British 'S' class submarines, launched between 1931 and 1937, had 6 internal bow tubes. Those launched between 1941 and 1945 had an external stern tube added. The 'T' class of 1937-41 were bigger submarines, with 10 tubes: 6 internal, 2 external in the bow and 2 external tubes amidships.

TORPEDO AND GUN

The torpedo was one of the most advanced weapons of World War II. Consisting of about 6,000 parts and weighing 1.5 tons, torpedoes were every bit as complicated as the submarines that fired them. A torpedo was, in fact, a miniature submarine, designed to make a single one-way submerged run at high speed (over 40 knots).

In a torpedo fuelled by compressed air and oil, only about one-fifth of its bulk was the explosive warhead. The remainder was taken up by the air tank, the engine, the gyroscope that kept the torpedo running straight, and the pendulum and depth-pressure valve that kept it running at the right depth.

Torpedoes driven by compressed air left a track of white bubbles in their wake. The most dangerous torpedoes, like the German electric and Japanese liquid-oxygen types, left no track that could be spotted in time.

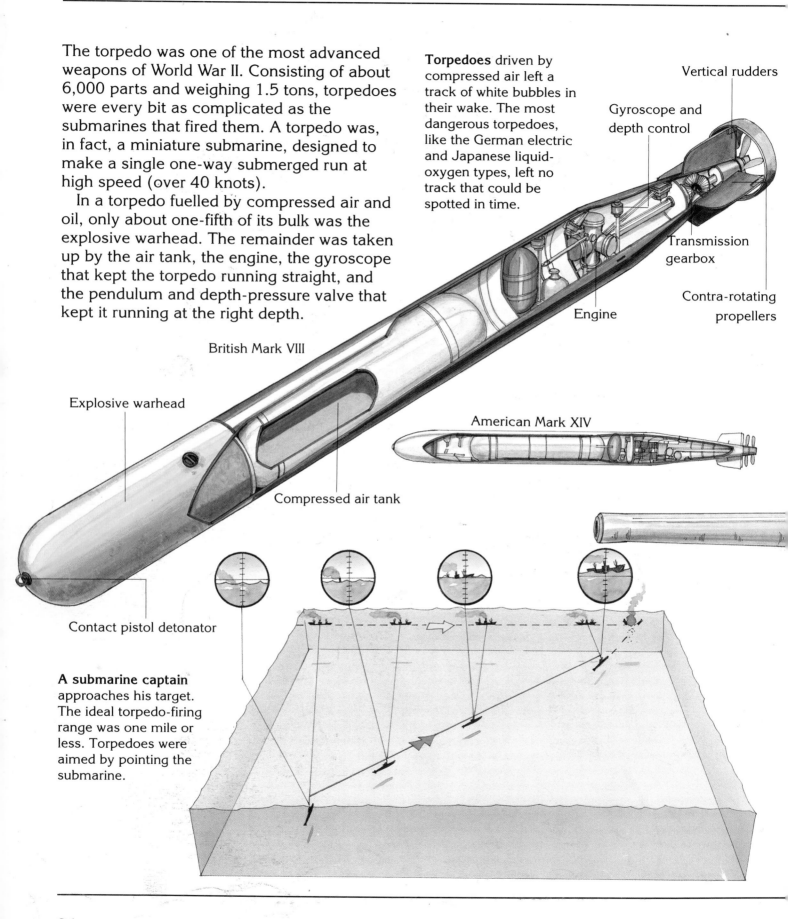

Vertical rudders

Gyroscope and depth control

Transmission gearbox

Contra-rotating propellers

Engine

British Mark VIII

Explosive warhead

American Mark XIV

Compressed air tank

Contact pistol detonator

A submarine captain approaches his target. The ideal torpedo-firing range was one mile or less. Torpedoes were aimed by pointing the submarine.

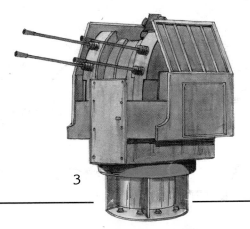

1. Rapid-firing ³/₄ inch Oerlikon gun – one of the most successful light anti-aircraft (AA) guns of the war. Fed by drum magazines, it fired over 460 small explosive shells per minute, and was fitted in almost every type of Allied warship, from battleships to submarines. The big American 'Gato' submarines did not have them; they had a single 1¹/₂ inch AA gun, the excellent 4³/₄ inch gun and 10 torpedo tubes.

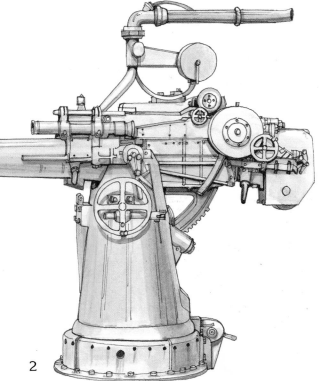

Apart from the heavy 4 inch guns of the ill-fated French submarine cruiser *Surcouf*, submarine guns varied considerably in caliber: the diameter of the shells they fired. The heaviest was the American 6 inch; the lightest was the British 3 inch. All had to be resistant to seawater. To help the barrel drain quickly after surfacing, the breech could be left open and the first shell loaded while water was still running out of the barrel. A good gun crew could get the first shell away within 45 seconds of the hatches being opened. By 1943, submarines were being fitted with at least one rapid firing small caliber gun for anti-aircraft defense.

2. World War I veteran: the British 3 inch gun, often jokingly called the 'anti-Zeppelin gun'.

3. In 1943 the Germans added a quadruple 20-mm anti-aircraft gun to their new U-boats.

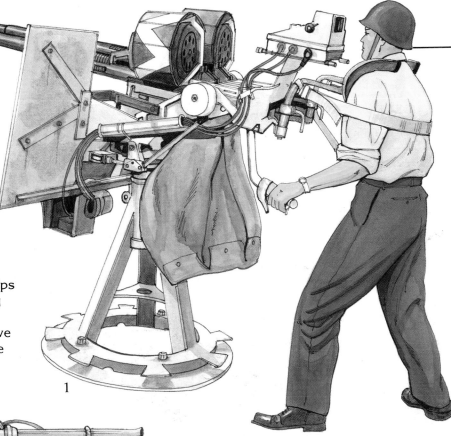

BATTLE OF THE ATLANTIC, 1940-43

1. Consolidated PBY Catalina flying boat, which U-boats came to dread. Allied aircraft saved many merchant ships merely by forcing U-boats to stay submerged.

After the German air force (*Luftwaffe*) failed to defeat the British RAF in 1940, the German navy (*Kriegsmarine*) tried to starve Britain into surrender by attacking merchant ship convoys in the North Atlantic. This was called the Battle of the Atlantic: the U-boat war. By early 1943, Germany had built enough U-boats to attack convoys in overwhelming strength. But the British and their allies had developed new weapons and tactics against the U-boats. The most important of these was the use of long-range aircraft that were able to bridge the 'Black Gap' in the mid-Atlantic, where the U-boats had earlier roamed out of reach of air attack.

In March 1943, 112 of Germany's 240 operational U-boats were sent against the Allied convoys. They sank 97 merchant ships, at a rate of 12 ships sunk for every U-boat destroyed. But the Allies fought back with more surface escort groups, trained in the teamwork of U-boat hunting, long-range air patrols which found U-boats on the surface by radar, and with escort aircraft carriers which could give constant air cover to convoys. May 1943 was decisive. The Allies sank 41 U-boats, compared with only 15 in March. The U-boat threat remained to the end of the war, but Germany had lost the Battle of the Atlantic.

2. Once located by sonar, the U-boat was attacked with depth charges. Here a charge is loaded onto its thrower.

3. The disposable thrower drops away as the charge is fired. Other depth charges were simply dropped from the ship's stern.

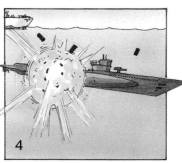

4. Though direct hits were usually fatal, even a near-miss could cause enough damage to force a U-boat to surface and be attacked.

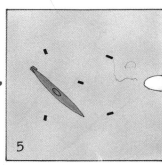

5. A typical depth charge pattern, dropped and thrown by the warship passing over the U-boat's estimated position.

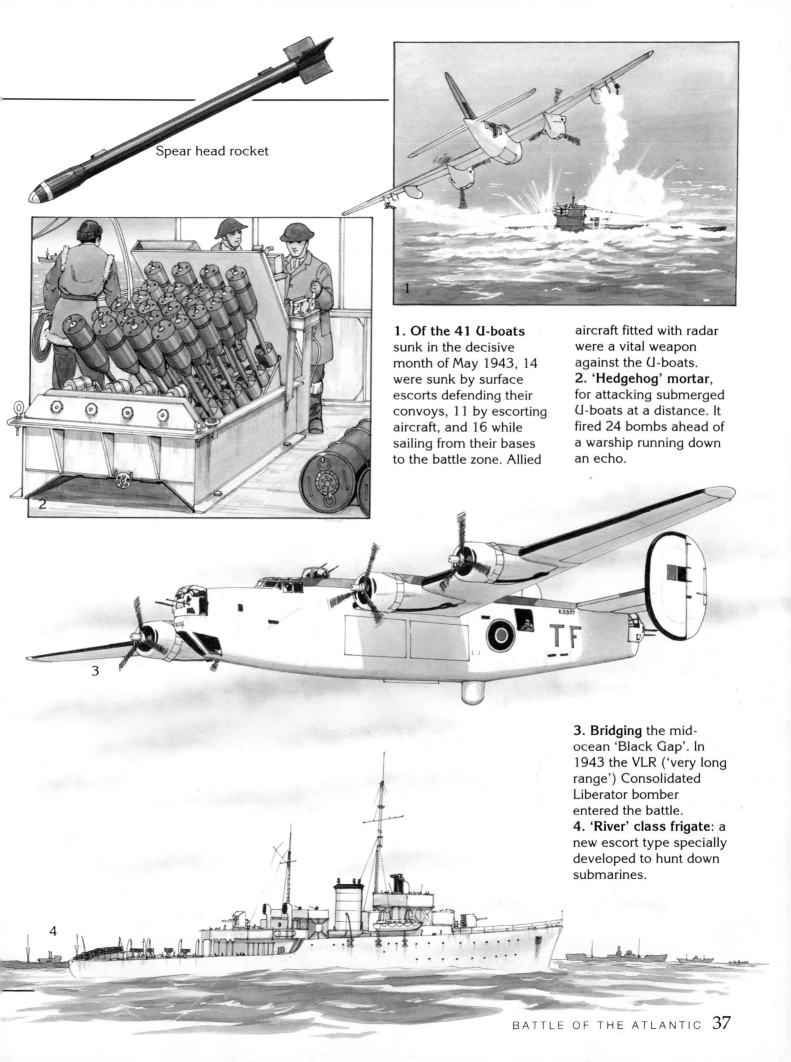

Spear head rocket

1. Of the 41 U-boats sunk in the decisive month of May 1943, 14 were sunk by surface escorts defending their convoys, 11 by escorting aircraft, and 16 while sailing from their bases to the battle zone. Allied aircraft fitted with radar were a vital weapon against the U-boats.

2. 'Hedgehog' mortar, for attacking submerged U-boats at a distance. It fired 24 bombs ahead of a warship running down an echo.

3. Bridging the mid-ocean 'Black Gap'. In 1943 the VLR ('very long range') Consolidated Liberator bomber entered the battle.

4. 'River' class frigate: a new escort type specially developed to hunt down submarines.

U-BOAT ATTACK

'Stragglers', merchant ships straying from the main body of their convoy, were easy meat for U-boats. This U-boat has sunk one straggler and is attacking another.

Whenever possible, the submarine captain did his best to help survivors get away in their boats, sometimes giving their position and course to the nearest land.

The U-boat war was especially brutal because no submarine had the space to take prisoners on board. Captains put the safety of their own ship and crew above that of torpedoed survivors.

Between 1939 and 1945, Germany built 1,170 U-boats of all types. Of these, 781 were lost in action and a few by accident. Another three were captured. One of these, *U-570*, was taken over by the British Navy and renamed HMS *Graph*.

The leading U-boat of the Battle of the Atlantic was the Type VIIC, which displaced 769 tons surfaced and 871 tons submerged. The Type VIIC's surfaced speed on diesel was 17 knots – much faster than most British convoy escorts in the early years of the Atlantic battle – and its submerged speed was 7.5 knots.

The U-boat's early successes were due to the simple fact that the British 'secret

The high surface speed of all ocean-going U-boats enabled them to overtake most merchant ships, whether in or out of convoy.

weapon' of sonar was useless against a submarine attacking on the surface. On a dark night, too, the low outline of a surfaced U-boat was almost impossible to see. But

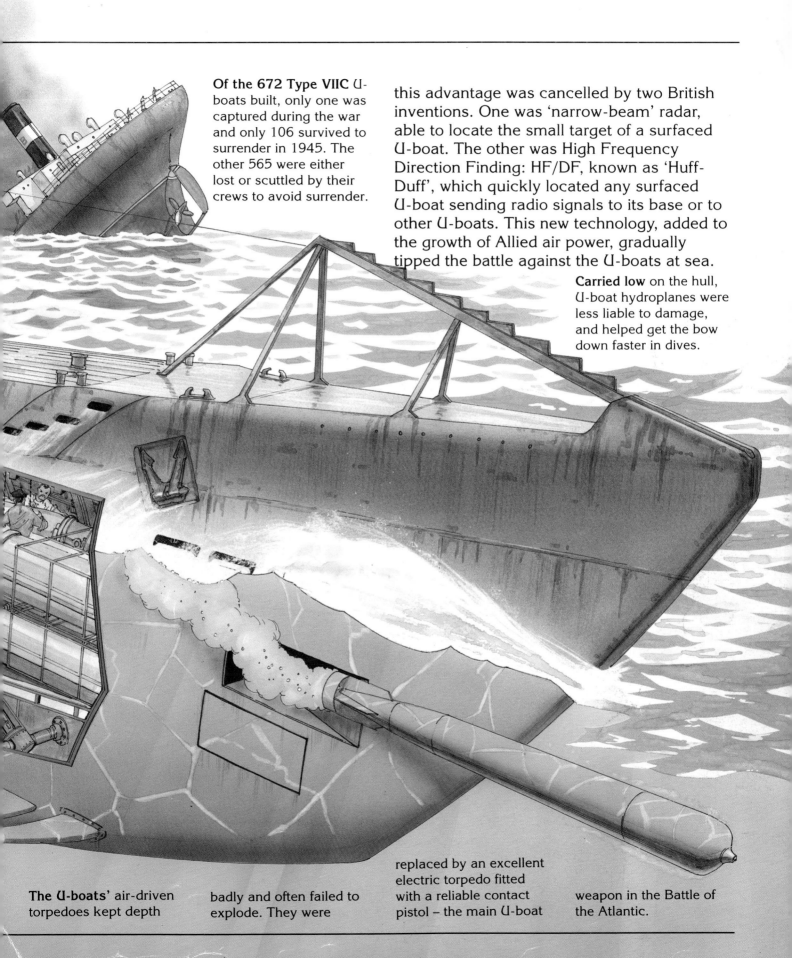

Of the 672 Type VIIC U-boats built, only one was captured during the war and only 106 survived to surrender in 1945. The other 565 were either lost or scuttled by their crews to avoid surrender.

this advantage was cancelled by two British inventions. One was 'narrow-beam' radar, able to locate the small target of a surfaced U-boat. The other was High Frequency Direction Finding: HF/DF, known as 'Huff-Duff', which quickly located any surfaced U-boat sending radio signals to its base or to other U-boats. This new technology, added to the growth of Allied air power, gradually tipped the battle against the U-boats at sea.

Carried low on the hull, U-boat hydroplanes were less liable to damage, and helped get the bow down faster in dives.

The U-boats' air-driven torpedoes kept depth badly and often failed to explode. They were replaced by an excellent electric torpedo fitted with a reliable contact pistol – the main U-boat weapon in the Battle of the Atlantic.

HUMAN TORPEDOES

1. Japanese A1 *Ha* 2-man midget submarine, driven by a 1-shaft electric motor. Because of the space taken up by its 2 internal torpedo tubes it had no engine to recharge its own battery, limiting its range to 92 miles at 2 knots.

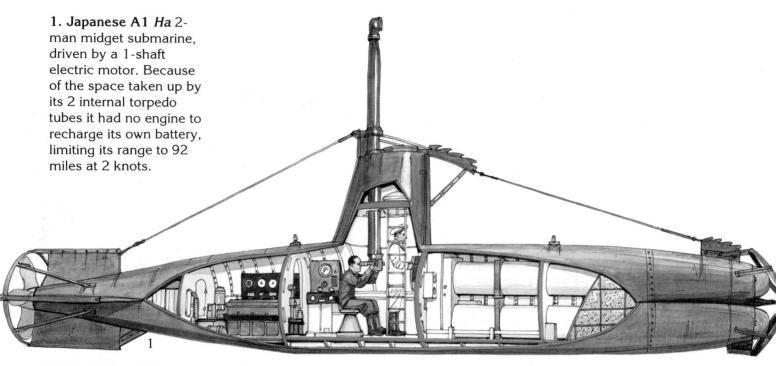

2. The Italian SLCs were nicknamed *maiali* ('pigs') by the brave men who rode them. Developed to attack British and French fleet bases, they had a few early failures before scoring a success: the attack on British battleships at Alexandria in December 1941.

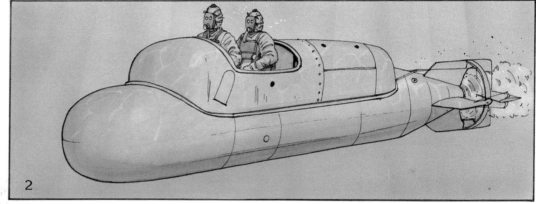

These special underwater attack craft were designed to get inside heavily defended harbors where ordinary submarines dared not venture. They had limited range, so most had to be carried or towed to within range of their targets by parent craft.

The first human torpedo was the Italian 'slow-speed torpedo' or *Siluro a lenta corsa* (SLC). After leaving its parent submarine it was steered into the enemy harbor. There the detachable warhead was fixed to the target and left to explode by a time-fuse while the crew escaped. Three SLCs made the most successful human torpedo attack of the war by badly damaging the British battleships *Valiant* and *Queen Elizabeth* in Alexandria on December 19, 1941.

The British human torpedo, known as the 'Chariot', succeeded in sinking the Italian cruiser *Bolzano* in June 1944.

Proper midget submarines were first developed by Japan. Torpedo-carrying A1 *Ha* boats got inside Pearl Harbor but failed to do any damage in December 1941. The best midget submarines of the war were the British X-craft. These crippled the German battleship *Tirpitz* in Kåfjord, Norway, in September 1943, and badly damaged the Japanese heavy cruiser *Takao* at its Singapore anchorage in July 1945.

3. British X-craft midget submarine. Instead of torpedoes they carried explosive charges, which were dropped under the target, and could also carry magnetic limpet mines. A special flooding chamber enabled a diver to leave the craft to cut through nets, or attach limpets to an enemy hull.

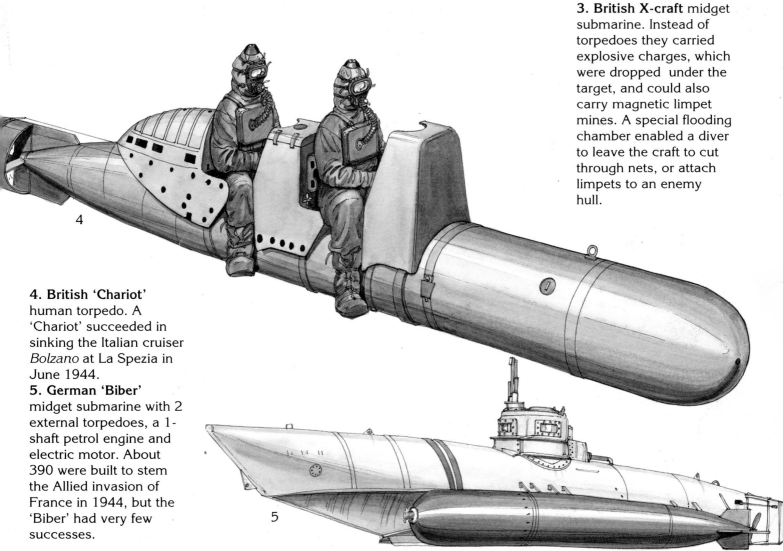

4. British 'Chariot' human torpedo. A 'Chariot' succeeded in sinking the Italian cruiser *Bolzano* at La Spezia in June 1944.

5. German 'Biber' midget submarine with 2 external torpedoes, a 1-shaft petrol engine and electric motor. About 390 were built to stem the Allied invasion of France in 1944, but the 'Biber' had very few successes.

MODERN SUBMARINES

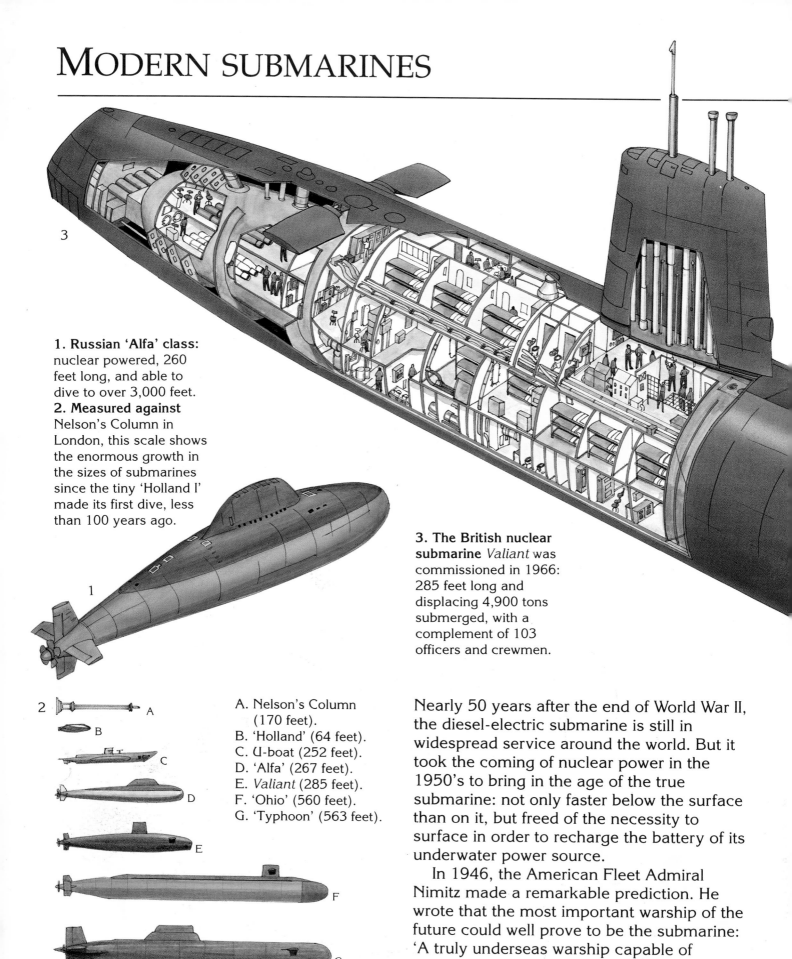

1. Russian 'Alfa' class: nuclear powered, 260 feet long, and able to dive to over 3,000 feet.

2. Measured against Nelson's Column in London, this scale shows the enormous growth in the sizes of submarines since the tiny 'Holland I' made its first dive, less than 100 years ago.

3. The British nuclear submarine *Valiant* was commissioned in 1966: 285 feet long and displacing 4,900 tons submerged, with a complement of 103 officers and crewmen.

A. Nelson's Column (170 feet).
B. 'Holland' (64 feet).
C. U-boat (252 feet).
D. 'Alfa' (267 feet).
E. *Valiant* (285 feet).
F. 'Ohio' (560 feet).
G. 'Typhoon' (563 feet).

Nearly 50 years after the end of World War II, the diesel-electric submarine is still in widespread service around the world. But it took the coming of nuclear power in the 1950's to bring in the age of the true submarine: not only faster below the surface than on it, but freed of the necessity to surface in order to recharge the battery of its underwater power source.

In 1946, the American Fleet Admiral Nimitz made a remarkable prediction. He wrote that the most important warship of the future could well prove to be the submarine: 'A truly underseas warship capable of circumnavigating the world without

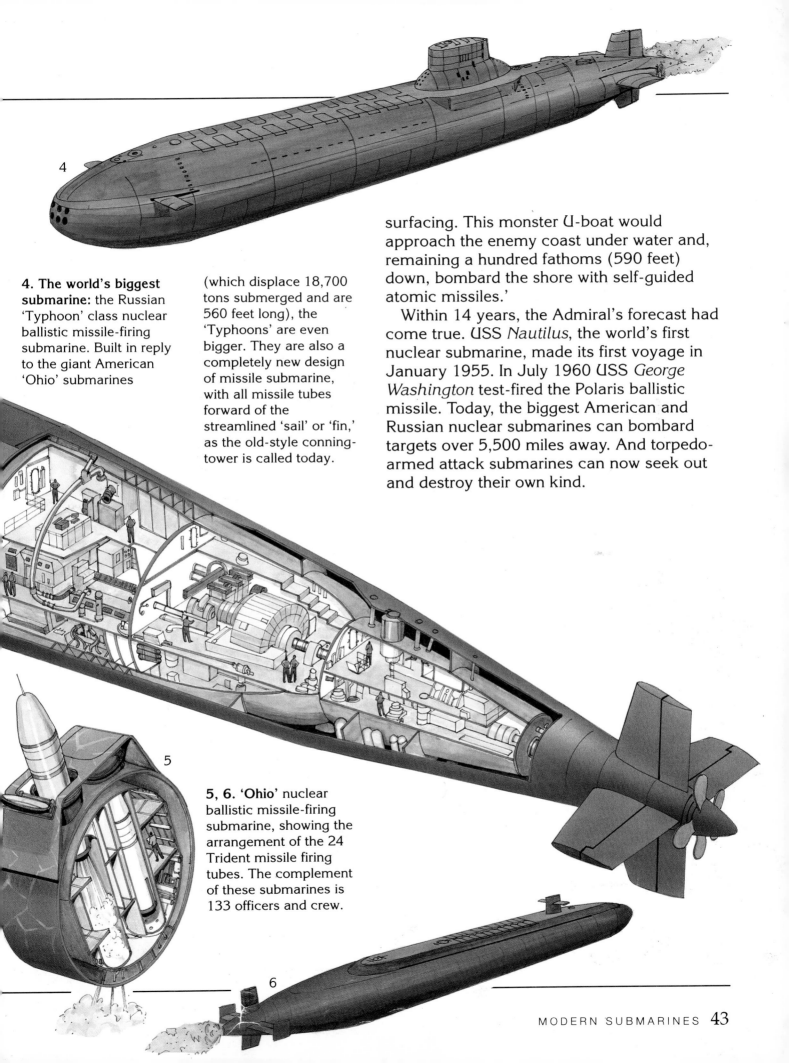

4. The world's biggest submarine: the Russian 'Typhoon' class nuclear ballistic missile-firing submarine. Built in reply to the giant American 'Ohio' submarines

(which displace 18,700 tons submerged and are 560 feet long), the 'Typhoons' are even bigger. They are also a completely new design of missile submarine, with all missile tubes forward of the streamlined 'sail' or 'fin,' as the old-style conning-tower is called today.

surfacing. This monster U-boat would approach the enemy coast under water and, remaining a hundred fathoms (590 feet) down, bombard the shore with self-guided atomic missiles.'

Within 14 years, the Admiral's forecast had come true. USS *Nautilus*, the world's first nuclear submarine, made its first voyage in January 1955. In July 1960 USS *George Washington* test-fired the Polaris ballistic missile. Today, the biggest American and Russian nuclear submarines can bombard targets over 5,500 miles away. And torpedo-armed attack submarines can now seek out and destroy their own kind.

5, 6. 'Ohio' nuclear ballistic missile-firing submarine, showing the arrangement of the 24 Trident missile firing tubes. The complement of these submarines is 133 officers and crew.

CHRONOLOGY

September 3, 1939 World War II breaks out.

September 14, 1939 The first U-boat, *U-39*, sunk.

September 17, 1939 British carrier *Courageous* sunk by *U-29*.

October 1940 First major U-boat successes in the Battle of the Atlantic: 63 Allied merchant ships (352,407 tons) sunk.

March 1941 British convoy escorts sink the three most successful U-boats in the Battle of the Atlantic: *U-47*, *U-99*, *U-100*. Otto Kretschmer, of *U-99*, is top-scoring U-boat 'ace' of the war, having sunk 44 ships (266,629 tons).

November 18, 1941 British battleships *Valiant* and *Queen Elizabeth* sunk in Alexandria by Italian 'human torpedoes'.

June 7, 1942 American carrier *Yorktown* sunk in Pacific by Japanese submarine *I-168*.

July 1942 U-boats sink 10 out of 34 ships of convoy PQ.17 to North Russia.

March 1943 Crisis point of North Atlantic battle: U-boats sink 12 merchant ships for every U-boat destroyed.

May 1943 Massive losses (44 U-boats sunk) win Allied victory in Battle of the Atlantic.

September 22, 1943 German ship *Tirpitz* crippled by British midget submarines.

June 19, 1944 Japanese carriers *Shokaku* and *Taiho* sunk by American submarines *Cavalla* and *Albacore*.

November 17, 1944 Japan's *Shinyo* sunk by American submarine *Spadefish*.

May 8, 1945 End of war with Germany; 156 surviving U-boats surrender, 221 are scuttled.

June 1945 Nine American submarines sink 27 merchant ships and Japanese submarine *I-122* in 11 days in Japan's Inland Sea.

July 31, 1945 Japanese cruiser *Takao* sunk by British midget submarine *XE-3*.

September 2, 1945 End of war with Japan.

SUBMARINE FACTS

1578 Englishman William Bourne suggested a warship that could submerge to escape from enemy cannon balls.

1620 Dutchman Cornelis Drebbel showed King James I of England a submersible boat, weighted down and rowed under the surface by 12 oars in watertight leather sleeves.

1804 The British refused to use Robert Fulton's submarine, 'which those who commanded the seas did not want and which, if successful, would at once deprive them of it.'

1866 Wilhelm Bauer's treadmill-powered *Diable-Marin* ('Sea Devil'), took a 4-man band to the bottom of Kronstadt Harbor to play patriotic tunes for the coronation of the new Russian emperor, Tsar Alexander II.

1901 Caged mice became pampered pets on board 'Holland' submarines, where they were kept to warn the crew when the air grew poisonous. The navy allotted the huge sum of one shilling per mouse per day for food and it was said the mice were usually too full of rum and grain to care if the air grew foul.

1902 British Admiral Sir Arthur Wilson called submarines 'underhand, unfair and damned un-English.' He said submarine crews captured in war should be hanged as pirates.

1915-18 Commander Arnauld de la Periere of the German Navy, with *U-35*, sank 189 merchant ships totaling 446,708 tons, becoming the most successful submariner of all time.

1917 British 'K-ship' submarines launched, powered by steam turbines with a surfaced speed of 24 knots – the fastest submarines until nuclear submarines were invented.

1939-40 So many U-boat torpedoes failed to explode that Karl Donitz, commander of the U-boat fleet, complained to Hitler that his men were 'having to fight with a dummy rifle.'

1941-45 American submarines, though representing only 2% of American naval strength in the Pacific Ocean, sank 240 Japanese warships and 2,200 Japanese merchant ships – over 91% of Japan's prewar merchant shipping fleet.

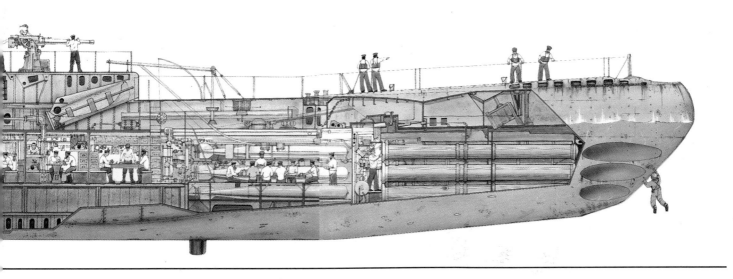

GLOSSARY

Amidships, the middle section of a ship.

Asdic (from the initials of 'Anti-Submarine Detection Investigation Committee'), the echo-sounding device for detecting submarines underwater, known today by the word sonar.

Ballast tanks, the tanks that are flooded with seawater to make a submarine dive, and pumped full of air to make it surface.

Bold, sonar decoy used by U-boats: a chemical 'pill' that, released into the sea, formed a mass of bubbles dense enough to return a sonar echo to hunting warships.

Bow caps, small doors at the outside ends of a submarine's torpedo tubes.

Breech, the strengthened rear end of a gun, hinged for loading shells and their propellant charges of explosive.

Caliber, the measurement of gun and shell size, taken from the internal diameter, or bore, of the gun barrel. Thus a 3 inch shell is not 3 inches long, but 3 inches in diameter.

Casing, a submarine's outer skin of light plating enclosing the ballast tanks and pressure hull.

Compensating tanks, internal tanks that are filled with adjustable levels of water to cancel the submarine's buoyancy, or tendency to float, during the achievement of a stable submerged trim.

Conning tower, (nowadays called the 'sail' or 'fin'), structure supporting the periscope standards and the bridge command position from which the submarine is directed or 'conned' while on the surface.

Contact pistol, torpedo detonator that explodes on striking a solid object.

Convoy, a group of merchant ships that sailed together with an escort of warships for greater protection against attack in time of war.

Depth charge (German *Wasserbomm,* or 'water bomb'), anti-submarine explosive charge, fused to explode at the estimated depth of the target submarine.

Displacement, the weight of a ship or boat, measured by the amount of water moved or displaced by placing the ship or boat in the water.

Engine clutch, the mechanical shift which, in a submarine, connects and disconnects each diesel engine from its propeller shaft.

Fairing, streamlined light structure or edge of plating.

Fitting out, installing the internal furnishings and fittings of a ship after launch to prepare the ship for active service.

Gyroscope, fast-spinning device whose weights and speed of rotation give stability to a steering device such as a compass.

Hatches, heavy watertight doors which, in a submarine, allow passage into and out of the pressure hull.

'Hedgehog' mortar, bomb-firing weapon carried by British anti-submarine warships to fire a cluster of 24 small bombs, fused to explode on contact, over the position of a submerged U-boat.

Helm, correct name for a ship's steering wheel.

Hydrophone, underwater listening device for detecting the sound of engines and propellers.

Hydroplanes, horizontal controls for adjusting a submarine's attitude in the water.

Jumping wire, heavy wire with cutting edge, stretched from bow to stern over the submarine's conning tower to cut or deflect underwater obstacles such as nets.

Limpets, explosive charges detonated by time-fuses, fixed to the hull of a target ship by means of magnetic clamps.

Magnetic pistol, torpedo detonator which explodes on passing through the magnetic field of a ship's steel hull.

Narrow-beam radar, a form of radar with a concentrated or narrow beam, designed for the location of small targets like surface submarines.

Neutral buoyancy, the stable condition of a submerged submarine correctly trimmed, neither rising nor sinking.

Periscope, retractable tube with reflecting prisms for viewing above the surface of the water from a submerged submarine.

Pressure hull, the main hull of a submarine, built with a circular cross-section for maximum strength to resist water pressure.

Rudder, hinged vertical control for lateral (left-right) steering.

Saddle tanks, arrangement of submarine ballast tanks on either side of the pressure hull.

Scuttling, the sinking of a ship by its own crew, to avoid its falling into enemy hands.

Snorkel (or German *schnorchel*), air-breathing tube to enable a submarine to run underwater on its diesel engines, developed for the German U-boat fleet in World War II.

Soda-lime, a chemical used to absorb moisture and carbon dioxide breathed into the air by the crew of a submarine during a long dive.

Sonar (from the initials of 'Sound Navigation and Ranging'), the word by which the Asdic echo-sounding system for locating submarines underwater is known today.

Tail clutch, the mechanical shift which, in a submarine, connects and disconnects each propeller shaft from its electric motor and diesel engine.

Torpedo tubes, fixed tubes from which a submarine's torpedoes are fired.

Trim, a submerged submarine's state of balance.

Trimming tanks, small tanks at either end of a submarine, between which water can be pumped to make adjustments to the trim.

U-boat (from the German *Unterseeboot*, or 'undersea boat'), term used for German submarines of the two world wars.

Vents, valves on top of the ballast tanks, opened to flood the tanks for diving, shut to blow the tanks full of air for surfacing.

Working-up, the time given for officers and crewmen to become fully accustomed to their new ship before sailing on their first war patrol.

INDEX

Note: page numbers in bold refer
to illustrations.